Rollover Mistakes Retirees Make

Rollover Mistakes Retirees Make

Eight Things You Need to Know Before You Roll Over Your 401(k)

Charles E. Winfrey Jr.

ISBN-13: 9780988621947
ISBN-10: 0988621940
Library of Congress Control Number: 2017901384
CL Publishing, Nashville, TENNESSEE

To my favorite people: Nancy Winfrey, Charles Everett Winfrey III,
Lauren Grace Winfrey, and Ernestine Winfrey

CONTENTS

PREFACE

On June 6, 1995, I began my life-long dream of working in the financial services industry at First American Bank here in Nashville, TN. The four years I spent at First American Bank prepared me for this journey I have traveled for the last eighteen years of assisting retirees and pre-retirees with their retirement income plans and goals. Since 1999, I have assisted thousands of individuals in avoiding the eight rollover mistakes that I share with you in this book. This book is not designed to be an exhaustive treatise on the subject of 401(k) rollovers but rather a preventative guide along your road to retirement confidence.

The ideas I share with you in this guide are based on eighteen years of real life situations, some that are probably similar to yours, that I feel can have a positive impact on your 401(k) rollover decisions. In fact, my desire to see every retiree and pre-retiree avoid these rollover mistakes is what led me to start The Rollover Company, Inc. over 15 years ago. At The Rollover Company, it is our mission and goal to help our clients avoid the rollover mistakes retirees make and we are committed to helping our clients build, protect and preserve their assets. Thank you in advance for reading my guide and I hope it helps you avoid these eight rollover mistakes retirees make. Before we begin this journey, please read the following disclosures.

or expressed herein. Your use of any information provided does not constitute any type of contractual relationship between yourself and the provider(s) of this information. The author hereby disclaims all responsibility and liability for all use of any information provided in this book. The materials here are not to be interpreted as establishing an attorney–client or any other relationship between the reader and the author or his firm.

Although great effort has been expended to ensure that only the most meaningful resources are referenced in these pages, the author does not endorse, guarantee, or warranty the accuracy, reliability, or thoroughness of any referenced information, product, or service. Any opinions, advice, statements, services, offers, or other information or content expressed or made available by third parties are those of the author(s) or publisher(s) alone. Reference to other sources of information does not constitute a referral, endorsement, or recommendation of any product or service. The existence of any particular reference is simply intended to imply potential interest to the reader.

The views expressed herein are exclusively those of the author and do not represent the views of any other person or any organization the author is or may be associated with.

ACKNOWLEDGMENTS

To my father, the late Rev. Dr. Charles E. Winfrey Sr., and my mother, Mrs. Ernestine S. Winfrey. I will add to what Abraham Lincoln said: "All that I am and all that I hope to be, I owe to my father and mother."

To my first love, my sixth-grade girlfriend, my bride, my soul mate, my partner in business, ministry, marriage, and parenting—Mrs. Nancy Annette Winfrey: thank you for your constant support, encouragement, belief, and love for the last twenty-plus years of our friendship and marriage.

To my firstborn, Charles Everett—the Lord knew I wanted a son, and he gave me my desire. As I write this book, I write with your future in mind. Do not make the same dumb financial decisions I made early in life, but rather take this book and others to lead you to a life of abundant wealth and opportunity.

To the apple of my eye, Lauren Grace, my daughter: you know you are Daddy's girl. Take this book and let it be the springboard to your financial destiny. As I said to your brother, do not make the same dumb financial decisions I made early in life, but rather take this book and others to lead you to a life of abundant wealth and opportunity.

To all of my clients for the last twenty-one years, thank you for your confidence, trust, and faith in me. I would not have the experience and knowledge to write this book without you allowing me to advise you.

A man must be big enough to admit his mistakes, smart enough to profit from them, and strong enough to correct them.
—JOHN C. MAXWELL

CHAPTER 1

ROLLOVER MISTAKE #1:
CLEANING OUT YOUR DESK AND YOUR 401(K)

A good decision is based on knowledge and not on numbers.
—*PLATO*

The day has finally come. For some of you, it has been thirty-plus years at one job, and you are ready to enjoy retirement. For someone else, it may be less than twenty years, and you are ready for a change. For another percentage of you, you may only have one to five years at your current employer, and a better opportunity has presented itself and you are changing jobs. No matter which category you fall in, the question still remains, "What do I do with my 401(k)?"

Do you keep it with your current company and its custodian? If you are permitted to, keeping it with your current company and plan allows you to continue your tax-deferred growth potential and broaden your protection of your assets from lawsuits; it may also keep your investment fees and expenses low. However, you can no longer contribute to the old plan. Sometimes your investment options are limited to less than fifteen investment choices in company-sponsored plans.

If you are changing jobs, do you roll it over to your new workplace plan if permitted? This option lets you consolidate your 401(k)s into one account, while continuing tax-deferred growth potential. However, as just stated, sometimes your investment options are limited, with less than fifteen investment options.

A third option may be to roll over your 401(k) to an IRA that allows you to consolidate your retirement accounts in one place, while continuing tax-deferred growth potential. With some IRAs, you have access to a wider range of investment options, but you could be limited in the accessibility of your funds depending upon your age.

The fourth option, which is the most common (and typically the most expensive) mistake I have seen over the last twenty-one years in retirement planning, is a retiree having his or her retirement account paid directly to him or her in the form of a check instead of rolling the funds over to a self-directed IRA.

Cashing out your 401(k), or in this case "cleaning out" your 401(k), is for many the worst mistake a retiree can make for the following reasons.

First, whenever you cash in your 401(k) instead of rolling it over, your former employer is required by law to withhold a mandatory 20 percent tax on your entire account balance. You will then have sixty days to deposit the cash, including the amount withheld, in a new tax-deferred retirement account before Uncle Sam keeps the 20 percent and you become responsible for any additional income tax due. If you are going to roll over an old 401(k), make sure that you always have the check made payable to the new custodian. As a general rule of thumb, when rolling over a 401(k), do not have the check made payable to yourself.

Second, if you are under the age of fifty-nine and a half and you do not roll over your 401(k), in addition to the 20 percent tax withholding, you will have an additional 10 percent early-withdrawal penalty added to your previous tax amount.

Finally, there is the opportunity cost you lose when you clean out your desk and your 401(k). *Opportunity cost* [1] refers to a benefit that a person could have received, but gave up to take another course of action. Stated differently, an opportunity cost represents an alternative given up when a decision is made. This cost is, therefore, most relevant for two mutually exclusive events. In investing, it is the difference in return between a chosen investment and one that is necessarily passed up.

When you sacrifice 20 percent (maybe 30 percent if you are under the age of fifty-nine and a half) of your retirement savings because you cashed out your 401(k) instead of rolling it over to an IRA, imagine how

1 Investopedia, "Opportunity Cost," http://www.investopedia.com/terms/o/opportunitycost.asp#ixzz4Tx3kA9eq, (December 10, 2016)

much more interest you could have earned if you did not give up those dollars.

In my professional opinion, the way to avoid this mistake is to have a plan. When I say a plan, I mean a retirement plan, not just a rollover plan. In the next chapter I explain the importance of having a retirement plan and not just a rollover plan.

CHAPTER 2

ROLLOVER MISTAKE #2:
HAVING A ROLLOVER PLAN, BUT NOT
A RETIREMENT PLAN

Most people don't plan to fail: they fail to plan.
—JOHN L. BECKLEY

The reason most people make the first mistake of cleaning out their desk and their 401(k) when they leave their employer is because they have a rollover plan but not a retirement income plan; not having such a plan is the second rollover mistake retirees make. Rollover planning is short-term thinking. Retirement income planning is long-term thinking.

When you have a rollover plan, your number one goal is getting access to the money you have inside your retirement account by any means necessary. The priority when you only have a rollover plan is gaining access to your money, while the potential taxes, penalties, and fees are not the focus. I have seen this happen time and time again when a retiree becomes anxious with the thought that "Now I am out on an island all alone managing money that in the past was handled by the custodian who managed my former company's retirement plan." There have been other times when a former company stipulates a timetable by which a retiree must make a decision of where to direct the account after retirement; this forces decisions to be made in haste. To prevent financial problems after retirement, it is important to have a retirement plan with five key components we will cover later in this chapter.

I believe all of us have pieces to our own retirement income puzzle (fig. 1). A puzzle is defined as a problem designed to amuse by presenting difficulties to be solved by ingenuity or patient effort. Having adequate retirement income is a problem that can be solved by patient effort in planning and preparing. I consider a 401(k) a piece to that retirement income puzzle, just as I consider savings, pensions, Social Security, IRAs, and real estate as pieces of that puzzle as well.

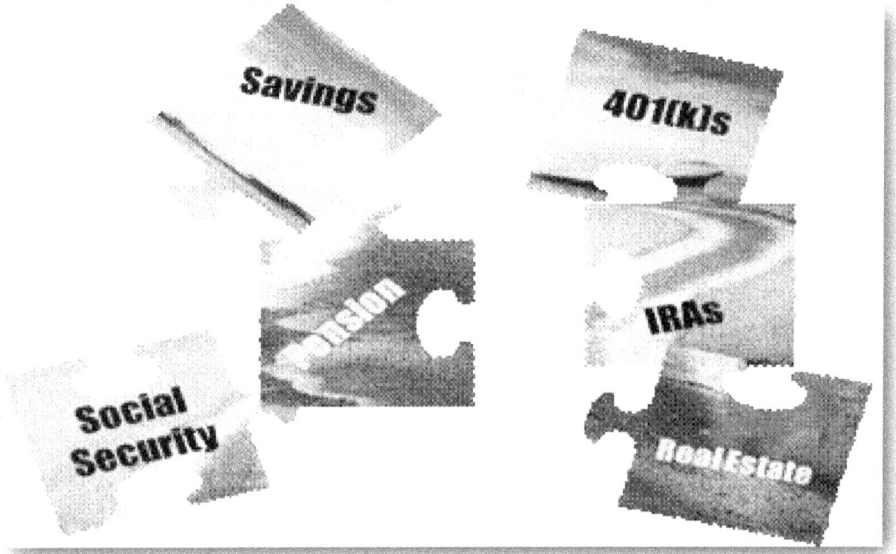

Figure 1. Retirement Income Puzzle

In working with retirees for the last twenty-one years, I have found that *most retirees have retirement income pieces, but they do not have a retirement income plan.* You will not and cannot solve your retirement income puzzle with scattered pieces; you only solve your retirement income puzzle when all of the pieces come together to complete your retirement income plan.

All the pieces of the puzzle working together as a retirement income plan include, but are not limited to, income and Social Security strategies, investments for liquidity and growth, and insurance products for income and protection. You need to diversify using investments that meet your risk tolerance and investment objectives. At the end of the day, it's simply about making your life and retirement work. This planning incorporates not just money, but also health care, long-term-care planning, and life insurance with a long-term-care rider, as well as legacy planning. Legacy planning is when you work with an estate planning attorney and your financial advisor to create and solidify a financial strategy for passing your assets to family, charities or other people specified in your will.

I believe that in order to have a completed retirement income puzzle, you need five key components. In my upcoming book *Retirement Confidence: How to Get It and Keep It*, I discuss in greater detail the five key components, but briefly let me cover them here in this chapter.

The first key component to a successful retirement income plan is an income plan. Every retiree needs an income plan that centers around how much income is wanted and needed in retirement. The most important part to your income plan is that the income you receive should be guaranteed lifetime income. In retirement, as was true while you worked, your income cannot change and should not change from month to month; rather, it should be guaranteed and paid to you for your entire life no matter how long you live after retirement.

The second key component to a successful retirement income plan is an investment plan. An investment plan is different from your income plan in that your investment plan will serve as a supplement to your income plan, but it is not the income plan. Many retirees lump their assets all into the investment plan and try to make their income plan and investment plan one; rather, they should stand alone. They have distinct purposes that work best separated, not combined.

The third key component to a successful retirement income plan is a health/life plan. Your health/life plan ensures that all of your bases are covered in the event of crisis. Adequate health, dental, vision, disability, long-term care, and life insurance are all critical to a completed retirement income puzzle.

The fourth key component to a successful retirement income plan is a tax plan. Having a tax plan for your retirement is an area where many retirees are ill prepared and are paying a hefty price for their lack of planning. Although at The Rollover Company we do not provide tax, accounting, or legal advice, we are able to work with your existing professional or refer you to a professional to aid you in these areas, as we know that they are integral to the success or failure of your retirement income plan.

The fifth key component to a successful retirement income plan is an estate plan. Estate planning is the act of preparing for the transfer of a person's wealth and assets after his or her death. Assets, life insurance, pensions, real estate, cars, personal belongings, and debts are all part of one's estate. Although we do not like to think about and dare not talk about death, it is a part of life and a part of your retirement income plan. Take the time, money, and effort to properly plan for the transfer of your assets at death so your heirs will not have to grieve and handle your estate at the same time.

Rolling over your money as quickly as you can without calculating the impact it will have on your retirement plan is one rollover mistake you cannot afford to make.

CHAPTER 3

ROLLOVER MISTAKE #3:
PUTTING ALL YOUR EGGS IN ONE BASKET

It is the part of a wise man to keep himself today for
tomorrow, and not venture all his eggs in one basket.
—MIGUEL DE CERVANTES

We have all heard many times over our lifetime "Do not put all your eggs in one basket." This piece of advice means that one should not concentrate all efforts and resources in one area, as one could then lose everything. But how is that a mistake for retirees with their 401(k)s?

In my professional opinion, all retirees have three needs that must be covered through planning and preparation. Those needs are emergencies, income, and lifestyle. I call these buckets the Trilateral Retirement Plan™.

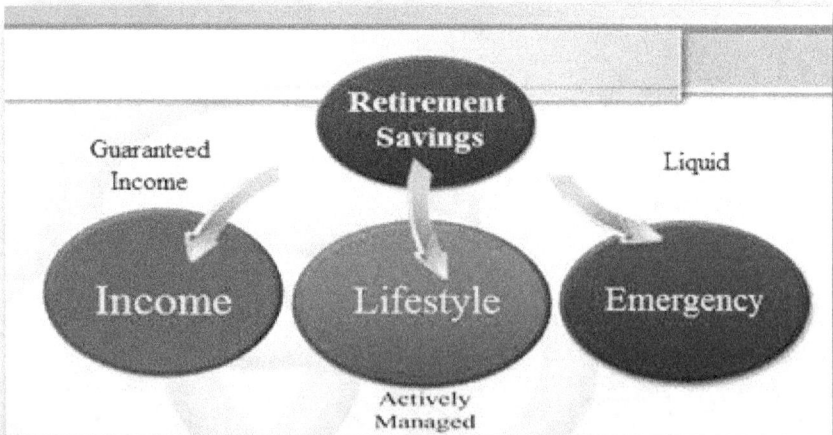

When retirees roll over their 401(k)s into only one basket, at least two of the three needs are not covered sufficiently and create potential dangers for the retiree. But why three baskets instead of one? Because you have three needs that must be met by three different means. Let us discuss bucket #1—Income.

The first rule of retirement is to guarantee consistent reliable income regardless of what is happening in the economy! The key to the income bucket is that the income generated for the retiree in retirement should be guaranteed lifetime income, income that provides you with the peace of mind that no matter how long you live, you will not outlive your money. This income also should keep pace with inflation. As the cost of living increases, your income should keep up with the rising costs and allow you to maintain your same standard of living. This income should provide for health-care costs as you age, and you should not have to worry about a major medical event derailing your retirement income. When you roll over your 401(k) into one basket, that basket may be designed to cover your current and future income needs, but how do you cover your emergency needs?

The second rule of retirement is to have enough funds to cover unexpected emergencies. No matter where you live, how old you are, and how well life is going right now for you, at some point life happens. Unexpected life situations happen that cause disruption in the normal day-to-day operations of your household and require resources to address those situations. That is why the second basket, for emergencies, is necessary so that when that time comes or that situation warrants immediate attention and resources, you have the resources to address the emergency immediately. When you roll over your 401(k) into one basket that may be designed to cover your current and future income needs but you also use it to cover your emergency needs, what about your lifestyle needs?

The third rule of retirement is having enough funds above your income and emergency needs to cover your lifestyle expenses. The lifestyle bucket is the bucket that provides the additional funds for you to have a lifestyle in retirement to travel, make necessary and desired purchases and gifts, and realize dreams you have deferred until retirement but without using the funds from your income or emergency buckets to cover those expenses. When the Trilateral Retirement Plan™ is established properly before you roll over your 401(k), it provides the RetirementConfidence™ you need by covering your income needs, emergency needs, and lifestyle needs.

Henry Ford has been credited for saying, "Put all your eggs in one basket and watch that basket." Mr. Ford's statement centered around the idea of being focused on your primary aim, not retirement income planning. Retirement income planning requires your attention and focus on your three financial buckets to ensure financial success in retirement. Remember, your three buckets are the income bucket, the emergency bucket, and the lifestyle bucket.

CHAPTER 4

ROLLOVER MISTAKE #4:
TAKING TOO MUCH RISK FOR YOUR AGE

> *If you take unacceptable risk, you have to*
> *be prepared to face the consequence.*
> —*CARLY FIORINA*

Risk[2] can be defined as the possibility of loss or injury. In regards to investing, risk can be defined as the chance an investment's actual return will differ from the expected return. Risk includes the possibility of losing some or all of the original investment. Risk is the potential to lose money permanently. The possibility of loss or that the investment's actual return will differ from the expected are enough words to conjure up the feeling that I could end up with less than I started with and less than I need in the long term. Although we know the definition and perils of risk, the fourth rollover mistake many retirees make is taking on too much investment risk.

One of the most basic principles of investing is to gradually reduce your risk as you get older, since retirees don't have the luxury of waiting for the market to bounce back after a dip. The dilemma is figuring out exactly how safe you should be relative to your stage in life. The solution to that dilemma is found in two strategies.

The first strategy is to complete a risk profile questionnaire (RPQ). Many retirees have never completed a risk profile questionnaire, or if

---

2 Investopedia, "Risk," http://www.investopedia.com/terms/r/risk.
asp#ixzz4TzEkFzmQ, (December 10, 2016)

they have, it was many years ago when they were younger and we lived in a different investment environment. But why is completing a risk profile questionnaire so important?

How you allocate your money among stocks, bonds, and short-term reserves may be the most important factor in determining the long-term return and volatility of your portfolio. The objective is to select funds only after you've determined the right asset allocation for you. A risk profile questionnaire makes asset allocation suggestions based on information you enter about your investment objectives and experience, time horizon, risk tolerance, and financial situation. As your financial circumstances or goals change, it may be helpful to complete the questionnaire again and to reallocate the investments in your portfolio. An RPQ is designed to help you decide how to allocate your assets among different asset classes (stocks, bonds, and short-term reserves). The allocations provided are based on generally accepted investment principles. There is no guarantee, however, that any particular asset allocation or mix of funds will meet your investment objectives. All investments involve risks, and fluctuations in the financial markets and other factors may cause declines in the value of your account. You should carefully consider all of your options before investing. The RPQ is designed to help you consider your risk tolerance. It asks questions that provide some indication of the risk tolerance for a typical investor displaying your personal investment characteristics (concerning investment and/or insurance products). It may not match your actual attitude toward investment risk, but it indicates the profile you fit into.

The second strategy to deal with the dilemma of determining how you should invest your retirement dollars is to understand the difference between returns and volatility.

Let's say you were given the choice to invest in two funds, Fund A or Fund B, and the only data you have on either fund is that for the last fifteen years (2000–2015) Fund A has averaged 5.66 percent per year with a Sharpe ratio of 1.91 percent, and Fund B has averaged 5.65 percent per year with a Sharpe Ratio of 0.21 percent. Which fund would you invest in? Probably this is not enough information to make an informed decision, right? What if I told you that Fund A was a well-known index fund and Fund B was a lesser-known fund, then which would you choose? More than likely you would choose the well-known index fund. But how do we know which fund performs better for our particular goals and objectives? We will answer this question from three hypothetical illustrations or scenarios.

In the first scenario, let's assume you invested $1,000,000 in Fund A starting in the year 2000 and $1,000,000 in Fund B starting in the same year, 2000. We will assume no additional funds were deposited nor were funds withdrawn from either account. As of December 31, 2015, which fund would you assume has the higher value: Fund A or Fund B? Actually, as of December 31, 2015, Fund B has an ending value $86,000 higher than Fund A. What made the $86,000 difference in Fund B compared to Fund A? Was it the commutative property of mathematics that says numbers in any order yield the same result? No, the difference is returns versus volatility. Let us go deeper in our understanding of the mistake of taking on too much risk.

In the second scenario, let's assume you purchased $1,000,000 worth of stock in another portfolio, which we will call Portfolio C, and $1,000,000 worth of a stock in another portfolio, which we will call Portfolio D, and you plan on investing in these two portfolios for only two years. How might volatility affect both Portfolio C and D?

Well, let's assume Portfolio C made 60 percent in Year 1, with a gain to your portfolio of $600,000, bringing your total after Year 1 in Portfolio C to $1,600,000. In Year 2, let's assume it lost 40 percent, reducing your value by $640,000, which brings your ending value down to $960,000 at the end of Year 2, with an average return of 10 percent.

Portfolio C-Hypothetical Illustration

Initial Purchase	$1,000,000.00
Year 1 Gain +60%	$600,000.00
Ending Value as of Year 1	$1,600,000.00
Beginning Value Year 2	$1,600,000.00
Year 2 Loss -40%	$640,000.00
Ending Value as of Year 2	$960,000.00
Year 1 Return	60%
Year 2 Return	-40%
Average Return in Two Years	10%

Now let us assume Portfolio D made 30 percent in Year 1, with a gain to your portfolio of $300,000, bringing your value after Year 1 in Portfolio D to $1,300,000. In Year 2, let us assume the portfolio lost 10 percent, reducing your portfolio value by -$130,000, which brings your value down at the end of Year 2 to $1,170,000. Both portfolios averaged the same 10 percent return after Year 2, but Portfolio D had a higher ending value. With that being said, if you would prefer to have the re-sults of Portfolio D, *you can live with low returns, but you cannot live with big losses.*

Portfolio D-Hypothetical Illustration

Initial Purchase	$1,000,000.00
Year 1 Gain +30%	$300,000.00
Ending Value as of Year 1	$1,300,000.00
Beginning Value Year 2	$1,300,000.00
Year 2 Loss -10%	$130,000.00
Ending Value as of Year 2	$1,170,000.00
Year 1 Return	30%
Year 2 Return	-10%
Average Return in Two Years	10%

Finally, let's return to our first two portfolios, Portfolios A and B. What would happen if you invested $1,000,000 in each portfolio and started receiving income of $50,000 per year in each portfolio from 2000 to 2015; which account would have a higher account value fifteen years later? According to our hypothetical illustrations, Portfolio B would, but how? From this simple concept: that volatility trumps returns. A low-volatility discipline may be the difference between retirement success and retirement failure.

Before I offered these three scenarios, we could have determined which account would fit your overall objectives better by analyzing the Sharpe ratios. A lower Sharpe ratio indicates the probability of a portfo-lio providing lower volatility in a turbulent market cycle.

Remember that the key to retirement income success is living with smaller gains instead of living with bigger losses. Since we learned from our hypothetical illustrations that volatility trumps returns every time, do not make the rollover mistake of taking on too much investment risk.

CHAPTER 5

ROLLOVER MISTAKE #5:
PAYING TOO MUCH IN FEES

A great company is not a great investment
if you pay too much for the stock.
—BENJAMIN GRAHAM

When deciding where to roll over your 401(k) upon retirement, you are typically given two options: a variable annuity or a mutual fund. My goal is not to convince you which option is better or worse; my goal is to educate you on the actual cost of investing in either of the two options.

Despite zealously monitoring the cost of items such as gasoline, groceries, and even wireless data plans, many Americans have no idea of the expenses in their investment accounts. According to a survey released in October 2014 by investment management firm Rebalance IRA, many Americans incorrectly believe they pay no fees in their retirement accounts. Rebalance IRA asked 1,165 baby boomers between ages fifty and sixty-eight, all with full-time jobs, how much they were paying in investment fees. Forty-six percent believed they paid nothing, and 19 percent were under the impression that their fees totaled less than 0.5 percent. In fact, according to data cited by Rebalance IRA, employees have retirement account expense deductions averaging 1.5 percent per year.

First, variable annuities. Variable annuities are often touted as a Swiss Army knife of investing. Salespeople will say this product can accomplish all your goals. But variable annuity fees can be as high as 3.00 percent or more per year. Higher fees means less of the investment returns come back into your account. These fees can make this one of the most expensive products that you can purchase. Take the time to understand all the following fees and charges before you buy.

Variable annuity fees fall into the following four categories:

Mortality expenses (M&E). This is a fee charged by the insurance company to provide you with a death benefit (often just a guarantee to pay out to your beneficiaries at least what was put in). This variable annuity fee can range from 0.50 to 1.5 percent of the policy value per year.

Administrative expense. Many variable annuity policies have a separate administrative fee to cover the cost of mailings and ongoing service. This fee can range from 0.10 to 0.30 percent of the policy value per year.

Investment expense ratio. Inside a variable annuity, the underlying stock and bond investment choices, called subaccounts, will have an investment management fee, which can range from 0.25 to 2.00 percent of the value in that account per year.

Additional cost of riders. Riders are extra features on your variable annuity policy that provide you with additional guarantees or death benefits. Depending on the extent of the benefit, riders can cost 0.25 to 1.00 percent of the policy value per year.

There are several key things to look out for with variable annuities. Within the variable annuity, there are the same investment options that you have outside of a variable annuity. If you are paying 3 percent or more a year in fees, your annuity has to earn back all the fees before you start seeing any return.

Annuities are insurance products, so take the time to understand what it is that you are insuring. Think of the annuity fees like an insurance premium. You are paying the insurance company to bear risk. They may be insuring your future retirement income by providing a guaranteed withdrawal benefit rider or insuring a specific amount of death benefit to go to your heirs or perhaps insuring a minimum return. Make sure you understand the benefits you are purchasing.

Let us move on to *mutual fund fees and expenses.* Fees are the shiny objects in the fine print of a mutual fund prospectus. Inevitably, investors' attention rivets on the expense ratio, which frames the ongoing cost of owning the fund, often to the exasperation of independent financial advisers. Here's what you need to know about that ratio, as well as lesser-known fees that affect the amount of money you reap for investing in a fund. Fees are important not only because they siphon money from your return, but because they are correlated with fund performance, In other words, funds with lower fees not only tend to cost less; they also tend to return more.

And make no mistake: you are paying a fee. It costs money to manage a fund. And *no-load* doesn't mean *free.* That is the biggest misconception about funds If you are in an employer-sponsored plan, don't rely on the bullet-pointed summary for all the key information. Take the time to research and read all fee-related details.

Those who do mine for fee information typically zero in on the expense ratio. That is the annual percentage of your money the fund management firm charges to manage the fund (including keeping that weighty prospectus up to date). A 1 percent expense ratio means the fund keeps one dollar for every one hundred dollars you have invested with it, every year. Most actively managed funds charge around 1 percent. A fund that is on algorithmic automatic pilot, such as an index fund, demands less human attention, so it might carry an expense ratio of 0.75 percent or much less. Either way, that doesn't sound like much, and that's the problem. The fee evaporates that sliver of money before you ever see it. The fees are there although you do not write a check and you do not see it on your statement. The average mutual fund, according to the Forbes[3] article entitled "The Real Cost of Owning a Mutual Fund," costs 3.12 percent per year.

In conclusion, beware of the seen and unseen fees you pay when rolling over your 401(k) into variable annuities or mutual funds.

---

3 Ty A. Bernicke, "The Real Cost of Owning a Mutual Fund," http://www.forbes.com/2011/04/04/real-cost-mutual-fund-taxes-fees-retirement-bernicke.html (April 4, 2011)

CHAPTER 6

ROLLOVER MISTAKE #6:
NOT UNDERSTANDING AND UTILIZING NET
UNREALIZED APPRECIATION

NUA can be a big tax savings or result in a big tax bill.
—*FIDELITY INVESTMENTS*

The sixth rollover mistake many retirees make is not understanding and applying NUA (net unrealized appreciation). If you own company stock in your 401(k) plan, there is a tax break that could save you a bundle on taxes—if you qualify. Anyone who owns company stock will eventually have to decide how to distribute those assets—typically when you retire or change employers. Taking a distribution could leave you facing a tax bill, but a little-known tax break—dealing with net unrealized appreciation (NUA)—has the potential to help. The way taxes are treated on net unrealized stock could provide benefits to a retiree who owns a large amount of company stock within their 401(k) that has significant appreciation.

What exactly is net unrealized appreciation? NUA is the difference between the price you initially paid for a stock (its cost basis) and its current market value. Say you can buy company stock in your plan for twenty dollars per share, and you use two thousand dollars to purchase one hundred shares. Five years later, the shares are worth thirty-five dollars each, for a total value of thirty-five hundred dollars: two thousand dollars of that figure would be your cost basis, and fifteen hundred dollars would be NUA.

Why should you care about NUA? When you want to distribute company stock or its cash value out of your 401(k), you will face a choice: roll it into an IRA, or distribute the company stock into a taxable account and roll the remaining assets into an IRA. The latter option might be more effective, depending on your circumstances, thanks to IRS rules governing NUA of company stock.

When you transfer most types of assets from a 401(k) plan to a taxable account, you pay income tax on their market value. But with company stock, you pay income tax only on the stock's cost basis—not on the amount it gained since you bought it. (If you are under age fifty-nine and a half, you may also pay a 10 percent early-withdrawal penalty.) When you sell your shares, you'll pay long-term capital gains tax on the stock's NUA. The maximum federal capital gains tax rate is currently 20 percent, far lower than the 39.6 percent top income tax rate, so your potential tax savings may be substantial. Depending on your MAGI (modified adjusted gross income), tax filing status, and net investment income, you may also owe a 3.8 percent Medicare surtax on net investment income. In this case, the maximum federal long-term capital gains tax rate becomes 23.8 percent.

If you have accumulated company stock in your employer-sponsored retirement plan, you may have several options when you're eligible to take a distribution from your plan. If the stock has appreciated significantly, you may want to consider applying the net unrealized appreciation (NUA) tax treatment. To do this, you take an in-kind distribution of some or all of your employer securities as part of a lump-sum distribution. This does not mean everything that is taken has to be a taxable distribution. Assets other than the portion of stock you are taking in kind can be rolled to an IRA, but there can be no assets remaining in the employer plan.

When you take an in-kind distribution of employer stock from your retirement plan, you generally pay tax on the cost basis (original value of the stock in the plan) of the securities at ordinary income rates in the year of the distribution. A 10 percent penalty may apply before age fifty-nine and a half. The shares are then held in a nonqualified brokerage account and are not taxed until you sell them. Any dividends you earn are taxable when they are paid, however. When you sell the shares, you will pay taxes at the long-term capital gains rate on any remaining net unrealized appreciation and the applicable capital gains rate on any additional appreciation since distribution. The applicable capital gains rate on any additional appreciation depends on the holding period after the distribution from the retirement plan. The advantage to the strategy is the difference between the ordinary income rate and the capital gains rate on any net unrealized appreciation that exists when you sell the stock.

NUA is not for everyone and makes most sense when the stock has appreciated considerably. For many people, an IRA rollover will make more sense than taking some or all of the employer stock as an in-kind distribution. Remember that it is risky to hold a significant portion of your retirement portfolio in one stock. If your former employer goes bankrupt, you will have paid tax up front for shares of stock that become worthless.

Let us review a case study to better understand the concept of net unrealized appreciation.

An executive in the 39.6 percent tax bracket decides to retire at age fifty. She holds one hundred thousand dollars worth of company stock, with a cost basis of twenty thousand dollars, resulting in NUA of eighty thousand dollars, and she wants immediate access to the cash.

She decides to distribute the assets into a taxable account and elect NUA tax treatment. She pays income tax and a 10 percent early-withdrawal penalty on just her $20,000 cost basis—a total of $9,920. She then immediately sells her company stock and pays 23.8 percent capital gains tax on the stock's $80,000 NUA. In all, she pays taxes and penalties of $28,960, leaving her with $71,040.

The assumptions in this case study are: (1) Company stock with a $100,000 market value, a $20,000 pretax cost basis, and NUA of $80,000 is distributed in kind from a 401(k) plan as part of a lump-sum distribution. (2) In the NUA scenario, the stock is immediately sold after being distributed from the plan; (3) in the rollover IRA scenario, the stock that was rolled over to the IRA is immediately sold, and the proceeds distributed in cash. (4) There is a 39.6 percent federal ordinary income tax rate on the $20,000 basis in the NUA scenario and on the entire

$100,000 in the IRA scenario. (5) There is a 20 percent federal long-term capital gains tax rate, plus a 3.8 percent Medicare surcharge, on the NUA in the NUA scenario. (6) The participant is subject to an early-withdrawal penalty of 10 percent on the $20,000 cost basis in the NUA scenario and on the entire $100,000 in the IRA scenario. State and local taxes are not taken into account. All the other nonstock assets distributed from the plan are assumed to be rolled over to a tax-deferred account to maintain their tax-deferred status and are not considered for purposes of this example.

Imagine she instead rolled her company stock into an IRA, then sold the shares and withdrew the cash. In that case, she would pay income tax and penalties on the entire $100,000, for a total of $39,600 in income tax and $10,000 in early-withdrawal penalties. As a result, she would wind up with just $50,400.

Please note that results will differ depending on an individual's holding period and percentage of NUA, but in this scenario, NUA tax treatment is clearly the better choice. The executive's high tax bracket and substantial NUA, both in absolute terms and as a percentage of her company stock's market value, enabled the NUA rule to produce considerable tax savings. If, on the other hand, the executive planned to wait fifteen years or more to tap her company stock, the full IRA rollover likely would have been more advantageous. Whether she left the company stock in the IRA or sold it to invest in other securities, her investments could have generated tax-deferred growth—which would probably eventually outweigh the NUA's initial tax savings.

The decision whether to take NUA treatment can be complicated. Certain situations may trigger restrictions on the NUA strategy. What's more, you should consider the way your distribution strategy affects your overall financial plan, including your estate plan, charitable giving, and perhaps most important, the level of diversification in your portfolio. A tax professional or financial adviser can help you determine whether the NUA rule applies to your individual circumstances and, if so, how best to deploy it. Please do not make the mistake many retirees make and just immediately roll over all of your company stock from your 401(k) into an IRA without understanding and applying the benefits of net unrealized appreciation.

CHAPTER 7

ROLLOVER MISTAKE #7:
MISUNDERSTANDING THE IN-SERVICE ROLLOVER

> *"Most of the trouble in life comes from*
> *misunderstanding, I think," said Anne.*
> — *L. M. MONTGOMERY,* ANNE OF THE ISLAND

Remember the good old days of whistling while you work in regards to your 401(k)? Your company used to have a very nice match to your 401(k). Your balance was at an all-time high, and retirement seemed like just over the horizon. Then 2008 came along, and the whistling turned into more of a whimper. Don't worry; I was whimpering, too. For those who are fifty-nine and a half and still working, I might have a reason for you to whistle again. The reason behind it is called the 401(k) in-service rollover. One of the biggest rollover mistakes retirees make is misunderstanding the in-service rollover. In fact, this book is probably the first time and place you have seen or read about this misunderstood concept. I want to assure you that you have not been hiding under a rock or not reading the 401(k) literature sent to you by your human resources department; most participants do not know nor have they heard of the in-service rollover.

An in-service rollover allows you to roll over your vested balance from your profit-sharing plan to an IRA while still employed. First, you will have to determine if you are eligible. I say that because some plans may restrict you from doing an in-service rollover. If you are eligible, here are some reasons that you might want to consider an in-service rollover.

Control—Who doesn't like control? With an IRA, you are the account owner and have more control over your assets, free from the restrictions your employer-sponsored plan can impose.

Diversification—Many employer-sponsored plans offer limited investment options. In contrast, most IRAs typically provide a wider range of investment choices across virtually every asset class. This flexibility can help you better diversify your retirement assets to meet your individual investment goals.

Beneficiary options—Typically, IRAs allow nonspouse beneficiaries to "stretch" an inherited IRA over their lifetimes. This type of beneficiary distribution option is not available in most employer-sponsored plans, which may limit distribution choices for your beneficiaries.

We have reviewed the benefits, but as in life, there are both advantages and disadvantages. Here are the disadvantages as to why you may not pursue an in-service rollover.

Age limitations—In qualified plans, the age fifty-five rule allows participants who stop working at age fifty-five or older to take distributions without the 10 percent IRS premature distribution penalty. In an IRA, you may not take distributions until age fifty-nine and a half. For this reason, if you plan to retire early, you may want to preserve penalty-free access to your retirement funds by not moving all of your 401(k) assets to an IRA before retirement.

NUA—Net unrealized appreciation (NUA) tax treatment, as we just discussed in chapter 6, is not an option for distributions from IRAs. Therefore, if you hold highly appreciated company stock in your employer-sponsored plan, the rolling of that stock to an IRA eliminates any ability you may have to take advantage of NUA tax treatment.

Creditor protection—While IRAs now have federal bankruptcy protection, other IRA creditor protection is still determined by state laws. Qualified plan assets continue to have broad federal creditor protection.

New contributions to your existing plan—Taking an in-service distribution may affect your ability to contribute to your employer-sponsored plan. Be sure to consult with your plan administrator before implementing this.

Cost—Fees related to having your own IRA could be more costly than the investment options inside the 401(k).

After-tax dollars—After-tax dollars are generally segregated in a qualified plan and can often be distributed separately. However, after-tax dollars complicate things if rolled to an IRA. If you move after-tax money into an IRA, that money becomes part of the nondeductible "basis" of the IRA and will not be separately accessible. To avoid paying tax again on your IRA basis when you take an IRA distribution, you must maintain careful records of the basis in your IRAs. This can become more of an issue in regards to doing a Roth IRA conversion.

We have reviewed the advantages and disadvantages; now we'll discuss how to know if you qualify.

First things first: you *have* to be fifty-nine and a half. No matter how much you dislike your current plan and you want to withdraw it all, an in-service rollover is not an option until then.

In-service rollovers don't apply just to 401(k)s. Thrift Savings Plans and 403(b) accounts are also available for the in-service rollover.

The in-service rollover is not for everyone and should be researched thoroughly before entering into, but for the right circumstances and people, it can make a huge difference in their retirement plan.

CHAPTER 8

ROLLOVER MISTAKE #8:
THE DIY ROLLOVER PROJECT

No man is an island entire of itself.
—JOHN DONNE

As I write this book, one of the most popular cable network channels is DIY TV. This channel was inspired to provide individuals who want to show themselves, their spouses, their coworkers or family members that they can fix the toilet, remodel the kitchen, and complete any project you can imagine by doing it themselves. In my professional opinion, one of the worst mistakes a retiree can make is undertaking a DIY rollover. A DIY rollover, like a DIY home project, can cost you time and a lot of money.

Not working with a financial adviser poses many risks to your financial future. When you want a job done right, you usually hire a professional to get the best results. The same can be said for managing your finances. While you may have some ideas about what types of investments to own, a financial adviser can offer you professional expertise and insight you may not have. Magazines, cable television, and websites produce a wealth of investing information on a daily basis, but do you really have time to evaluate it all to make the best investment decisions?

If you're a new investor, a financial adviser can help you determine the proper asset allocation to fit your lifestyle. If you currently have an investment portfolio, a financial adviser can evaluate your existing investments and determine if they are still appropriate for meeting your short- or long-term goals.

Remember, a financial adviser has time, knowledge, research tools, expertise, and experience you may not have. After all, investment planning is his or her full-time job.

Successful retirement, in my opinion, is the ability to replace current income in retirement. On average, Americans are on track to replace only 61 percent of their income in retirement. This number is increased for those who work with an adviser, save at least 10 percent of their salary, and have access to an employer-sponsored savings plan.

Why is the DIY rollover project a mistake? When you work with a retirement income adviser, his or her expertise and experience helps you avoid the eight most prevalent rollover mistakes.

Retirement income advisers will work with you to avoid the 20 percent mandatory tax withholding that occurs when you clean out your 401(k) when you leave your employer—much like your desk. A retirement income adviser should take you through the five key components needed to complete the retirement income puzzle as I summarized in Chapter Three, to determine if a rollover is the right move for you or not. If it is the right move, then that retirement income adviser will help you construct your retirement plan, not just a rollover plan.

Retirement income advisers will take you through the five key components needed to have a completed retirement income puzzle: the income plan, investment plan, health/life plan, tax plan, and estate plan.

That is why the DIY rollover project creates unnecessary stress, frustration, and potential issues. I encourage you to seek out a retirement income adviser who can assist you in making the right decisions when it comes to rolling over your 401(k).

CHAPTER 9

CONCLUSION

For the last twenty-one years, I have been assisting individuals, families, business owners, and nonprofits achieve their financial goals. I would like to do the same for you if you have the need.

I am here to serve. I am here to help you achieve financial success. If there are areas you need assistance in, please do not hesitate to contact our office. I thank you for the opportunity to share my ideas, thoughts, and insight. I look forward to hearing from you soon.

Stay connected with me:

Website: www.rollovercompany.com
Facebook: CharlesWinfreyJr
LinkedIn: Charles-Winfrey

ABOUT THE AUTHOR

As the senior adviser at the Rollover Company, Charles Winfrey is focused on helping clients work toward their retirement dreams through a well-thought-out strategy for retirement income.

Charles got his start in the industry in 1995, working for First American Bank, where he served as a personal banker until he moved to John Hancock Financial Services in 1999. Then in 2001, after realizing there was a better way to assist those preparing for retirement, he started his own company. His business philosophy is simple: to help clients increase cash flow and net worth, while also minimizing the taxes they incur.

Charles holds life and health insurance licenses in Tennessee, Georgia, Mississippi, Alabama, Virginia, Texas, and Maryland. He has also received his Series 65 securities license. He has a bachelor of business administration degree in finance from the University of Memphis.

He is a member of the National Association of Insurance and Financial Advisors (NAIFA) and has been recognized in the 2013 *Nashville Business Journal*'s 40 Under 40 list. He has used his financial acumen to assist the Lane College Board of Trustees and the local chapter of the Boy Scouts of America.

Charles was lucky to find love at an early age, as he married his sixth-grade sweetheart, Nancy. Together they have two children, Everett and Lauren. They reside in Nolensville, Tennessee.

In his free time, Charles enjoys traveling, writing, reading, and spending quality time with his family.

www.ingramcontent.com/pod-product-compliance
Lightning Source LLC
LaVergne TN
LVHW021548080426
835509LV00019B/2914